Dedicated to my dear father, Peter,
who also valued quiet observation, nature,
hard work, and making things by hand.

Many thanks to the Estate of Ruth Asawa,
The Josef and Anni Albers Foundation, and The Merce Cunningham Trust
for their guidance and contributions to this book.

Published by
Princeton Architectural Press
A division of Chronicle Books LLC
70 West 36th Street, New York, NY 10018
papress.com

Printed in China
25 24 23   9 8 7

ISBN: 978-1-61689-836-6

Published by arrangement with Debbie Bibo Agency

This book was illustrated with charcoal and colored pencil drawings
combined with hand-painted and monoprinted paper.

Editors: Rob Shaeffer and Parker Menzimer
Designer: Andrea D'Aquino

Special thanks to:
Paula Baver, Janet Behning, Abby Bussel, Jan Cigliano Hartman,
Susan Hershberg, Kristen Hewitt, Stephanie Holstein, Lia Hunt, Valerie Kamen,
Jennifer Lippert, Sara McKay, Wes Seeley, Sara Stemen, Marisa Tesoro,
Paul Wagner, and Joseph Weston of Princeton Architectural Press
—Kevin C. Lippert, publisher

Library of Congress Cataloging-in-Publication Data
available upon request.

A LIFE MADE by HAND

THE STORY OF
RUTH ASAWA

ANDREA D'AQUINO

PRINCETON ARCHITECTURAL PRESS • NEW YORK

This is the story of an artist
you may have never heard of.

Her name is Ruth Asawa.

She was born in California,
and her whole family worked on a farm.

Working with her hands was an ordinary thing to do.
It was what all the hardworking people around her did.

But Ruth was no ordinary person.

Ruth looked carefully at everything around her.
"What kind of plant are you?" she wondered.

"What a fascinating shape   your shell is, Snail."

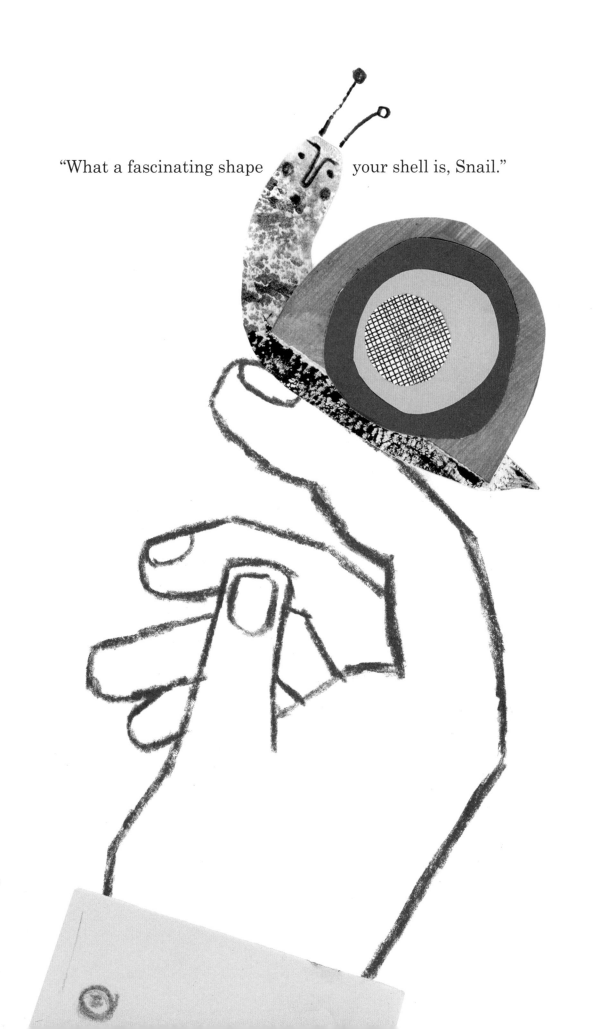

"What delicate and beautiful wings you have, my friend!"

"Hello
Spider.
How did
you figure
out how
to make
your
web?"

Ruth liked to look
at the drops of water
in her garden.
She often stopped
to notice how the
light shone through
their delicate shapes.

Her hands were always busy making
things out of anything she could find.

She made tiny animals out of the wire
she found around the farm.

She created shapes by folding paper.

She loved to draw forms in the dirt with her bare feet.

On Saturdays, Ruth got a break from busy farm work.
Her parents sent her to Japanese school where she
was given lessons in calligraphy.

She learned to hold the paintbrush and shape
the bold characters with black ink.

When Ruth was older she continued to study art. She went to
Black Mountain College, an unusual school filled with brilliant people.

People like choreographer Merce Cunningham,
who made shapes in the air with dancers' bodies.

And one of her most inventive teachers, Buckminster Fuller, who was always busy coming up with new ideas to make our planet a better place to live.

scientist

designer

inventor

author

futurist

poet

mathematician

architect

philosopher

visionary

Josef Albers taught students
to make art out of everything
around them.

Leaves! Paper! Wire! Clay!
Even garbage—
don't throw it away.

Just look at it in a new way.

He became famous for
his square color paintings.

Ruth was eager to learn from interesting people around her. On a trip to Mexico, a local craftsman taught her how to weave with wire, looping it around and around to make baskets.

When Ruth got back home,
she experimented with wire.

She was so excited to
discover that   a line can go anywhere.

In Ruth's hands, simple wire
turned into graceful sculptures
that were light as air.

Ruth continued to weave all day, even when she had a family of her own around her.

Her hands never stopped moving as she looped and looped, over and over again.

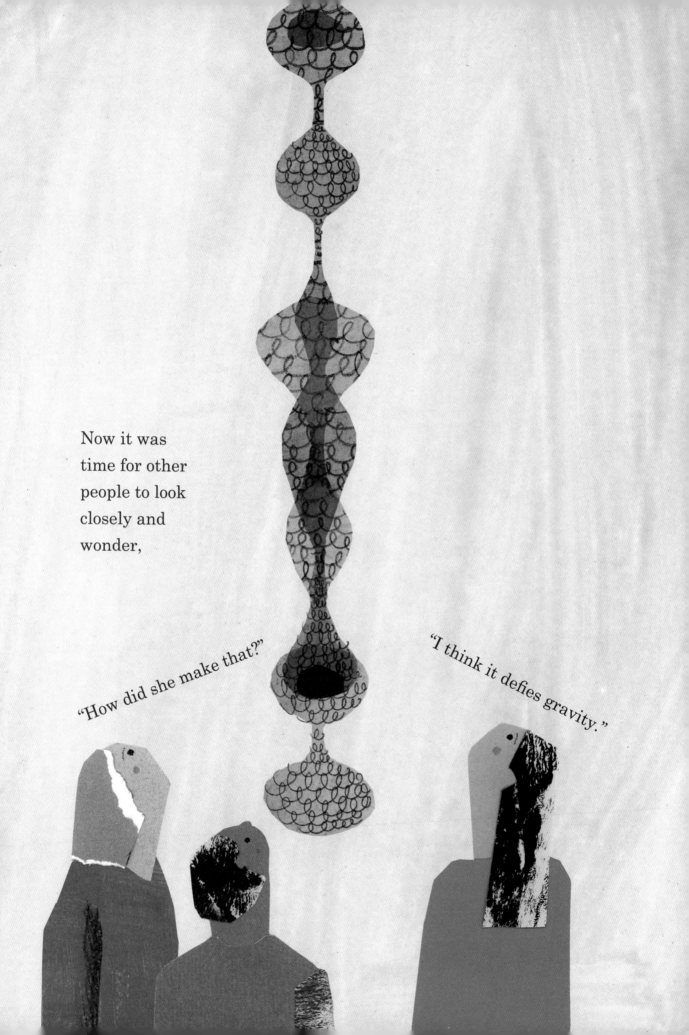

Now it was
time for other
people to look
closely and
wonder,

"How did she make that?"

"I think it defies gravity."

"Is it some kind of sea creature?"

"Maybe something from outer space!"

The one
thing everyone
knew was that her
sculptures were
beautiful.

People go to see Ruth's art in museums
all around the world. You can too.

AUTHOR'S NOTE

Like so many, I found seeing Ruth Asawa's sculptures in person to be a powerful experience. I discovered that her respect for the natural world and dedication to all things handmade resonated deeply with my own experiences in becoming an artist.

I'm honored to have had the opportunity to speak in-depth with Asawa's daughters, Aiko Cuneo and Addie Lanier, who oversee the Estate of Ruth Asawa. They pushed me to a deeper understanding of their mother and her joyful spirit. Asawa acknowledged the profound impact of her mentors at Black Mountain College and felt that her growth as an artist was deeply rooted in their philosophies.

The time is overdue for Asawa's contributions to twentieth-century art to be considered on their own merits, not only in context of her life story. I have honored her family's wish that this book celebrate Asawa's life without allowing the darker facts of her internment to overshadow her art. That history is addressed below, so that it may be given the appropriate weight in a deeper conversation that the topic so deserves.

MORE ABOUT RUTH ASAWA

Ruth Asawa was born on January 24, 1926, in Norwalk, California. She was one of seven children in a family that earned its living doing farm work. Growing up, Asawa and her siblings attended a Japanese school on Saturdays to learn the language and culture of their heritage.

In February 1942, in response to Japan's attack on a US naval base at Pearl Harbor, the American government instituted a program of incarceration for people of Japanese ancestry. Approximately 120,000 Japanese Americans were removed from their homes on the West Coast and forced to live in internment camps. Over 70,000 were American citizens. The government started by sending active Japanese American community leaders, including Asawa's father, to a detention center in New Mexico.

A few months later, Asawa and the rest of her family were forcibly relocated to the Santa Anita Racetrack in Arcadia, California. While there, she met and studied with three Walt Disney illustrators and co-internees. By the fall of 1942, her family was moved to an internment camp in Rohwer, Arkansas. In September 1943, Asawa was released from the camp in order to attend college in Milwaukee, Wisconsin. Her three older siblings were released to study at colleges in Iowa. Her parents and two younger siblings were released in November 1945. Asawa continued to pursue her art, and was encouraged by friends to study at Black Mountain College in North Carolina. Its faculty included Josef and Anni Albers, Merce Cunningham, John Cage, and Buckminster Fuller. The college attracted many artists, including Robert Motherwell, Franz Kline, Milton Avery, Elaine de Kooning, Cy Twombly, Robert Rauschenberg, and Jacob Lawrence.

While attending Black Mountain College, Asawa met her future husband, Albert Lanier, an architecture student at the time. They married in 1949, after Asawa completed her studies. The couple settled in San Francisco where they raised their six children.

Besides working on her art and raising a family, Asawa was very active in introducing arts education to public schools. In 1968, she co-founded the Alvarado School Arts Workshop. It brought professional artists into the classroom to teach art, gardening, music, and theater. The workshop eventually spread throughout San Francisco's public schools. In 1982, Asawa helped found a public high school for the arts, later renamed the Ruth Asawa San Francisco School of the Arts. In 2009, Ruth's Table, a center for creative learning, was founded at the Bethany Center in San Francisco. Its mission is to foster opportunities for people of all ages to engage in creative expression.

Ruth Asawa passed away in her San Francisco home in 2013, at the age of eighty-seven.

RESOURCES

www.ruthasawa.com
www.ruthstable.org

Ruth Asawa: Life's Work
by Aruna D'Souza, Helen Molesworth, and Tamara Schenkenberg

Densho Encyclopedia
An online resource on the history of Japanese American incarceration

Fred Korematsu Speaks Up: Fighting for Justice
by Laura Atkins and Stan Yogi (YA title)

Black Mountain College: Experiment in Art
by Martin Brody and Vincent Katz

Leap Before You Look: Black Mountain College 1933–1957
by Ruth Erickson and Helen Molesworth

"Sculpture is like farming. If you just keep at it, you can get a lot done."

—RUTH ASAWA

Remember the insect that Ruth
studied when she was a girl?

Now you can make one!

Ruth was a teacher, and
knew that the best way to
learn is to use your hands.

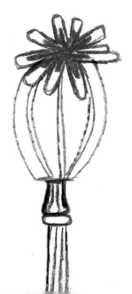

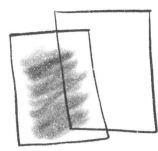

1. Choose 2 sheets of paper in different colors and glue them back to back.

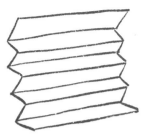

2. When dry, fold accordian-style. This one is folded 7 times.

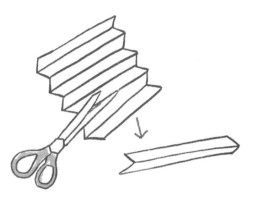

3. Cut off the bottom section to make a small strip with just 1 crease in it.

4. Flatten the folds to make wings. Press down on the center and spread out each side.

5. Fold the small strip in half to make the insect body.

6. Wrap the body around the wings and glue or tape it down. Draw a face on it, or whatever else you think of.

You did it!
It's okay if yours looks different.
That's what makes each one special.

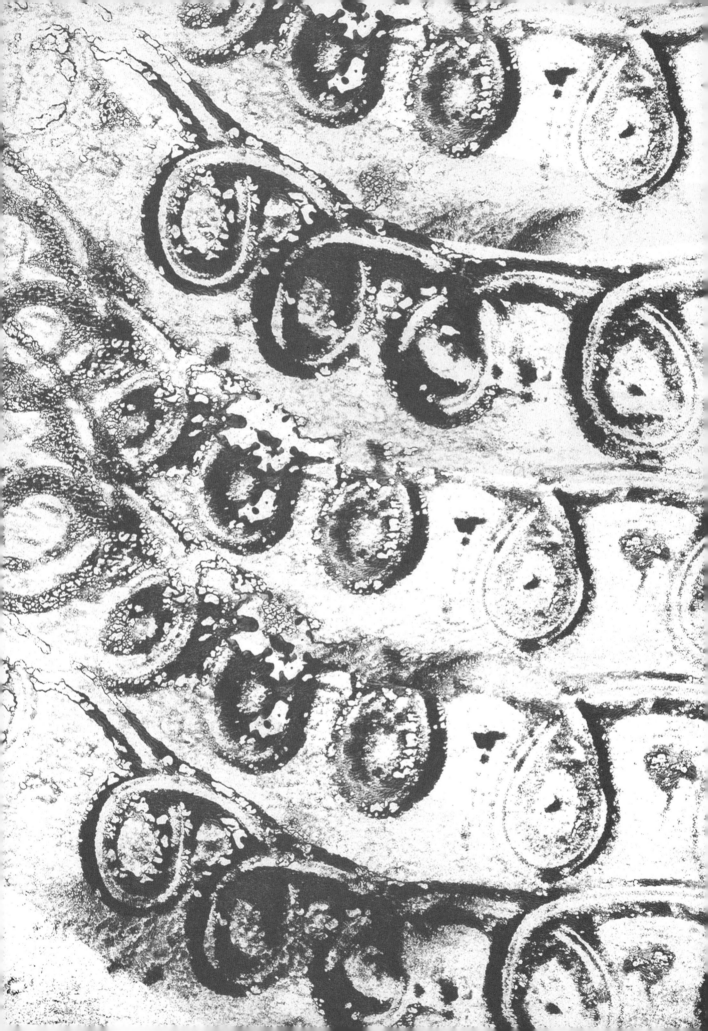